GURU GRANTH SAHIB

An Insight into the Format and Design

A special release on the 400ᵗʰ anniversary of the first installation of Guru Granth Sahib

Dr. Sukhbir Singh Kapoor
Vice Chancellor, World Sikh University, London

&

Mrs. Mohinder Kaur Kapoor, M.A.

Hemkunt

© Hemkunt Publishers (P) Ltd.

First Published 2004

ISBN 81-7010-335-5

Published by:

Hemkunt Publishers (P) Ltd.
A-78, Naraina Industrial Area, Phase-I, New Delhi-110 028
Tel.   :   2579-2083, 2579-5079, 2579-0032 • Fax: 91-11-2611-3705
E-mail   :   hemkunt@ndf.vsnl.net.in
Website :   www.hemkuntpublishers.com

Printed at: Sita Fine Arts Pvt. Ltd., 25896999

This book is dedicated to:

*The Students Union - World Sikh University, London
for their love and dedication to their studies.*

&

The Sadh Sangat wherein God himself lives.

OTHER BOOKS BY THE SAME AUTHOR

All books are in English; Gurubani text, where relevant, is both in Panjabi and English.
Year of publication/book list

2004
1. Sikh Law Book – The Law personally handed by God to Guru Nanak

2003
1. Guru Granth Sahib – An Advance Study Volume 2
2. Dasam Granth – An Introductory Study
3. Comparative Studies of World Religions. (Second edition)
4. Asa di Var – an epic the listening of which fulfils all worldly desires.

2002
1. Guru Granth Sahib – An Advance Study Volume 1
2. Sikh Religion and the Sikh People (Third revised edition)
3. Sikhism – An Introduction (Second revised and enlarged edition)
4. Japji – A way of God realisation (Third edition)

2001
1. Sikhism – 1000 questions answered
2. Guru Granth Sahib – An introductory Study (enlarged edition)
3. Sikh Philosophy, Facts and Fundamentals of Sikh Religion (2nd edition)
4. Japji – The Sikh morning prayer (Illustrated deluxe edition)

2000
1. Bhagat Bani
2. Sikh Religion and the Sikh People (2nd edition) *'Adjudged best book of the year'*

1999
1. Sikhism – An Introduction
2. Saint Soldier (The Khalsa Brotherhood)
3. Comparative Study of World Religions
4. The Creation of Khalsa (Edited)
5. Japji, "A way of God realisation" (2nd edition) *'Adjudged one of the best available translation in English'*

1998/97
1. Guru Angad Dev, Life, History and Teachings
2. Nitnem (The daily Sikh Prayers) (Translation in both easy Panjabi and English)
3. Khushi de Hanju – (ਖੁਸ਼ੀ ਦੇ ਹੰਝੂ) Panjabi poetry

1996
1. The Sikh Marriage Ceremony (Anand Marriage)
2. Baramah (The twelve months)

1995
1. Kirtan Sohila and Ardas
2. Gurbani – God's Word
3. Jap Sahib, Swayas and Ardas, Master compositions of Guru Gobind Singh Ji (Translation followed by relevant Sakhis (life stories))
4. Janoon – (ਜਨੂਨ) Panjabi poetry

1994/93
1. Rehras & Kirtan Sohila – "The torch to pass through the darkness of death, and the Lyric that speaks of lacerations and pangs of separation." (Translation followed by relevant Sakhis (life stories))
2. Sikh Philosophy, Facts and Fundamentals of Sikhism (1st edition)
3. Puniya da Chand – (ਪੁਨਿਆ ਦਾ ਚੰਨ) Panjabi poetry

1992/91
1. Japji (1st edition)
2. Sikh Religion and the Sikh people (1st edition)

1990
1. Being a Sikh

1989/88
1. Ideal Man, Guru Gobind Singh's Concept of a Saint Soldier

1984
1. Invasion of Golden Temple

1983
1. Sikh Festivals

1982
1. Sikhs & Sikhism

Introduction

It is an amazing coincidence that our generation had the divine blessings to   celebrate the 300th birth anniversary of Guru Gobind Singh (1966), the 500th birth anniversary of Guru Nanak (1969), the 300th birth anniversary of the Khalsa (1999), the 500th birth anniversary of Guru Angad (March 2004) and now the 400th anniversary of the first installation of Guru Granth Sahib (September 2004)

We have already published three titles on Guru Granth Sahib:

Guru Granth Sahib - An Introductory Study
Guru Granth Sahib - Advanced Study Volume I
Guru Granth Sahib - Advanced Study Volume II

We are pleased to release two new books on the subject as an ode to the triumphant legacy of the Sikh Nation to commemorate the 400th anniversary of the first installation of (Guru) Granth Sahib:

An Insight into the Format and Design of Guru Granth Sahib, and
The Sikh Law Book

Our thanks are due to our publication secretary Ms Poonam Kapoor for her support and help in producing this volume.

Dr. Sukhbir Singh Kapoor
Mrs. Mohinder Kaur Kapoor
London
23rd January 2004
released on 31st August 2004

The Basic Sikh Doctrine (Prayer)

Ik ongkar satnam kartapurkh nirbhau nirver akalmurat ajuni sebhang gurparsad

ੴ ਸਤਿ ਨਾਮੁ ਕਰਤਾ ਪੁਰਖੁ ਨਿਰਭਉ ਨਿਰਵੈਰੁ ਅਕਾਲ ਮੂਰਤਿ ਅਜੂਨੀ ਸੈਭੰ ਗੁਰ ਪ੍ਰਸਾਦਿ

O Lord God you are the sole Master of the Universe. You lived in all ages and times. You are the source of all Cosmic Energy. You are the Creator and manifest in your Creation. You are the Sovereign and all powerful (you have no fear). You are Benevolent and Merciful (You have no enmity). You are Eternal and Immortal (You yourself are beyond death). You are the Cause of births and deaths and you yourself are not entangled in them (You are not born). You are Self Illuminated and Self Revealing. It is Your Grace which gives us health, wealth and prosperity. So be it.

Word Meaning

The syllables	The meaning
Ikongkar is made up of three syllables: Ik + Ong + Kar	Ik = God is one, the whole universe has one God Ong = One who has no parallel. Who is the Saviour of the universe. Kar = He is the sole Designer of the universe and has been there in all eras. He was there before the start of time, he was there when the time had started, he is there now and he will always be there in all the times to come.
Satnam is made up of two syllables Sat + Nam	Sat = Truth, unchangeable, permanent Nam = Cosmological Energy, power He is the Truth and source of power of the whole cosmology.
Kartapurkh is made up of two syllables Karta + Purkh	Karta = the Creator Purkh = Omnipresent He is the only Creator and is omnipresent
Nirbhau is made up of two syllables Nir + Bhau	Nir = devoid of Bhau = fear He is devoid of all fears viz., the fears of death,

	destruction, loss of power, loss of status, loss of treasures, loss of kith and kin etc.
Nirver is made up of two syllables Nir + ver	Nir =devoid of Ver = enmity He is devoid of enmity. He looks after good and bad alike. He supplies provisions to the whole creation even to a tiny insect which lives in stones.
Aakal is made up of two syllables Aa + kal	Aa = Beyond, not Kal = death He is beyond death. He is immortal and has lived in all ages and time periods.
Aajuni is made up of two syllables Aa + juni	Aa = Beyond, not Juni = birth, lives He is beyond births. He is not born/made of procreation processes
Sebhang is made up of two syllables Se + bhang	Se = self Bhnag = illuminated He himself started the pendulum of the time. He is self illuminated
Gurparsad is made up of two syllables Gur = parsad	Gur = God himself Parsad = Grace All our possess are with His blessings and Grace. (*To invoke His blessing we must pray, meditate and do noble deeds*)

The two hymns read on the day of the first installation of Guru Granth Sahib in 1604

It is belived that the following hymns were the first compositions to be read on the day of the installation of the Adi Granth, in Harimandir (Golden Temple) on 31st August 1604

1. Pauri (Stanza) 20, Var Srirag Mehla 4 (page 91)

ਪਉੜੀ ॥ ਕੀਤਾ ਲੋੜੀਐ ਕੰਮੁ ਸੁ ਹਰਿ ਪਹਿ ਆਖੀਐ ॥ ਕਾਰਜੁ ਦੇਇ ਸਵਾਰਿ ਸਤਿਗੁਰ ਸਚੁ ਸਾਖੀਐ ॥ ਸੰਤਾ ਸੰਗਿ ਨਿਧਾਨੁ ਅੰਮ੍ਰਿਤੁ ਚਾਖੀਐ ॥ ਭੈ ਭੰਜਨ ਮਿਹਰਵਾਨ ਦਾਸ ਕੀ ਰਾਖੀਐ ॥ ਨਾਨਕ ਹਰਿ ਗੁਣ ਗਾਇ ਅਲਖੁ ਪ੍ਰਭੁ ਲਾਖੀਐ ॥ ੨੦ ॥

Pauri: Whatever work you wish to accomplish—tell it first to God. He will resolve your affairs; the true teacher gives His guarantee of Truth. In the company of the holy people, you shall taste the treasure of the ambrosial nectar. God is merciful and dispeller of all fears; He preserves and protects His devotees. O Nanak, sing the glorious praises of God, and see the unseen God in your own heart. ‖ 20 ‖

2. Raga Suhi, Mehla 5, page 783

ਸੂਹੀ ਮਹਲਾ ੫ ॥ ਸੰਤਾ ਕੇ ਕਾਰਜਿ ਆਪਿ ਖਲੋਇਆ ਹਰਿ ਕੰਮੁ ਕਰਾਵਣਿ ਆਇਆ ਰਾਮ ॥ ਧਰਤਿ ਸੁਹਾਵੀ ਤਾਲੁ ਸੁਹਾਵਾ ਵਿਚਿ ਅੰਮ੍ਰਿਤ ਜਲੁ ਛਾਇਆ ਰਾਮ ॥ ਅੰਮ੍ਰਿਤ ਜਲੁ ਛਾਇਆ ਪੂਰਨ ਸਾਜੁ ਕਰਾਇਆ ਸਗਲ ਮਨੋਰਥ ਪੂਰੇ ॥ ਜੈ ਜੈ ਕਾਰੁ ਭਇਆ ਜਗ ਅੰਤਰਿ ਲਾਥੇ ਸਗਲ ਵਿਸੂਰੇ ॥ ਪੂਰਨ ਪੁਰਖ ਅਚੁਤ ਅਬਿਨਾਸੀ ਜਸੁ ਵੇਦ ਪੁਰਾਣੀ ਗਾਇਆ ॥ ਅਪਨਾ ਬਿਰਦੁ ਰਖਿਆ ਪਰਮੇਸਰਿ ਨਾਨਕ ਨਾਮੁ ਧਿਆਇਆ ॥ ੧ ॥

Suhi Mehla 5: God himself has stood up to resolve the affairs of the holy; He has come to complete their tasks. The land is beautiful, and the pool is beautiful; within it is contained the ambrosial water. The ambrosial water is filling it, and my job is perfectly complete; all my desires are fulfilled. Congratulations are pouring in from all over the world; all my sorrows are eliminated. The Vedas and the Puranas sing the praises of the perfect, unchanging, imperishable primal Waheguru. The transcendent Waheguru has kept His promise, and confirmed His nature; Nanak meditates on the Nam, the name of God. ‖ 1 ‖

Contents

Contents

The Holiest Book Containing the Word of God — Guru Granth Sahib

The name of the Sikh holy scripture is **Guru Granth Sahib**. It is made up of three syllables which mean:

Guru = The Ultimate teacher, God, Waheguru

Granth = A holy book

Sahib = An epitome of reverence

Brief history of the Compilation of Guru Granth Sahib

Guru Nanak wrote his hymns in a notebook, later called **Guru Harshai Pothi,** and he passed it on to Guru Angad, when he himself left for the heavenly abode.

Guru Angad added his own hymns in this pothi and passed it on to Guru Amardas.

Guru Amradas instructed his grandson Sahasar Ram to put all hymns of Guru Nanak, Guru Angad and himself in a definite order and prepare edited pothis (books). These pothis were called **Mohan pothis** or **Goindval Pothis.**

Guru Ramdas wrote his own hymns and passed on his **collection** directly to Guru Arjan.

Guru Arjan then collated all hymns of the first four Gurus and added with them his own compositions. He prepared a large voluminous Granth, called it **Pothi Sahib** and put it at a higher pedestal. It took him four years 1601-1604 to complete the Granth. Bhai Gurdas was the scribe of this Granth. This Granth had its first official Parkash Divas (opening ceremony) on 31st August 1604 in the newly constructed Gurdwara named Harimandir (the house of God, now known as Golden Temple) at Amritsar.

In 1706 while staying at Damdama Sahib, Guru Gobind Singh asked Bhai Mani Singh to rewrite the Granth adding therein the hymns of the ninth Guru. In 1708, at Nanded, Guru Gobind Singh conferred the title of Guru on the Granth Sahib and ended the line of human Gurus. He re-titled Granth Sahib as Guru Granth Sahib.

The Authorship and the Revelation Recipients

It is believed that God speaks to us whenever we need Him, only the recipient has to be clever enough to understand the message.

Sikhs believe that the author of Guru Granth Sahib was God himself. He revealed his words to the Sikh Gurus who in turn conveyed the message to the people at large through the *Shabad.*

Guru Arjan then selected compositions of a few Bhagats (Saints) and other devotees, to whom God had also revealed his word and whose compositions were in line with the Sikh ideology. He included these hymns with the hymns of the Sikh Gurus and put them together in (Guru) Granth Sahib. The list of all composers, their time period and number of hymns selected for inclusion in the Granth, is as follows:

Table 1
The Sikh Gurus

The Guru	Domicile	Time period (Life)	No. of hymns
Guru Nanak	Punjab	1469 - 1539	974
Guru Angad	Punjab	1504 - 1552	63
Guru Amardas	Punjab	1479 - 1574	907
Guru Ramdas	Punjab	1534 - 1581	679
Guru Arjan	Punjab	1563 - 1606	2218
Guru Tegh Bahadur	Punjab	1621 - 1675	115

Table 2
The Bhagats

The Bhagat	Domicile	Time period (life)	If coincides with the Guru period	Religion/caste	No. of hymns
Kabir	Uttar Pradesh	1398 - 1495	Yes	Hindu/low caste - weaver	541 (including 243 sloaks)
Farid	Punjab	Born 1173	No	Muslim	134 (including 130 sloaks)
Namdev	Maharashtra	Born 1270	No	Hindu/low caste – calico printer	60
Ravidas	Uttar Pradesh	15th Century	Yes	Hindu/low caste - chamar	41
Dhanna	Rajasthan	Born 1425	Probably yes	Hindu/ Jat	4
Tirlochan	Maharashtra	Born 1267	No	Hindu/ Vaish - Arora	4
Beni	Uttar Pradesh	—	NA	—	3
Bhikhen	Uttar Pradesh	16th Century	Yes	Muslim	2
Jaidev	Bengal	12th Century	No	Hindu/ High caste – Brahmin	2
Parmanand	Maharashtra	Not known	NA	Hindu/ High caste – Brahmin	1
Pipa	Maharashtra	Born 1425	Probably yes	Hindu/ High caste - Rajput	1
Ramanand	Uttar Pradesh	Born 1359	No	Hindu/ High caste - Brahmin	1
Sadhna	Sind	13th Century	No	Hindu/ low caste - butcher	1
Sain	Madhya Pradesh	14-15th Century caste - barber	Probably yes	Hindu/low caste	1
Surdas	Uttar Pradesh	Born 1528	Yes	Hindu/High caste - Brahmin	1

Table 3
Other Devotees (their time period coincides with the Guru period)

The devotee	Domicile	Time period (life)	Religion/caste	No. of hymns
Mardana	Punjab	1459 - 1520	Muslim	3 sloaks
Satta	Punjab	16th Century	Muslim	1 var
Balwand	Punjab	16th Century	Muslim	Co-author of var with Satta
Sundar	Punjab	16th Century	Sikh	1 six pada shabad

Table 4

Bhatts (They were all Brahmin and hailed from Karnal. They composed Swayas to introduce the Guru-composers to readers at large. Bhatts' count differs from author to author due to the similarities of their names. Many authors have counted them as 17)

Name of the Bhatt	Swayas to Introduce Guru Nanak	Swayas to Introduce Guru Angad	Swayas to Introduce Guru Amardas	Swayas to Introduce Guru Ramdas	Swayas to Introduce Guru Arjan	Total Swayas of the Bhatts
1. Kal	10			16		26
2. Kalshar		10	9	13	12	44
3. Jalap			5			5
4. Kirat			4	4		8
5. Bhikhey			2			2
6. Sal			1	2		3
7. Bhal			1			1
8. Gayandh				13		13
9. Mathura				7	7	14
10. Bal				5		5
11. Harbans					2	2
Total	10	10	22	60	21	123

The Language of Guru Granth Sahib

The script of Guru Granth Sahib is called Gurmukhi. However, the languages used in compositions are many in number. It is due to the following basic reasons:

1. Guru Nanak travelled almost every known corner of India, he also visited many foreign countries viz., Ceylon, Bangladesh, Tibet, China, Afghanistan and Middle East. Many of his hymns have stamp of local dialects, of the places he visited, on them viz., Arabic, Persian, Sindhi, Multani, Lehndi, Hindi etc. Guru Arjan's compositions also have effect of these languages.

2. The Bhagats had different domicile, this invariably effected their compositions. Thus their compositions have words of Marathi, Bengali, Braj, Persian and many other minor dialects.

Most of the compositions of Guru Angad, Amardas and Guru Ramdas are in Eastern Punjabi. Guru Tegh Bahadur's compositions are a mixture of Punjabi and Hindi.

In addition to the above languages, many hymns are composed in *Sant Bhasha*, which was a mixture of many languages and was used by roaming saints to compose their hymns.

Segment 5

The Subject Matter of Guru Granth Sahib

The Subject matter of Guru Granth Sahib includes the following:
1. God, His curriculum vitae, His domicile and methods of His realisation.
2. The meaning and modes of worship.
3. The methods used for God Manifestation
4. The Sikh law
5. Ethics and rules of living a truthful life.
6. The theory of Creation
7. The Concepts of :
    a. Nam
    b. Guru
    c. Satguru
    d. Nirankar
    e. Waheguru
    f. Sadh-sangat
    g. Sins
    h. Virtues
    i. Sorrows
    j. Happiness
    k. Love
    l. Hate
8. The human and divine relationships and their significance.
9. Theory of Karma and God's Grace
10. The life after death
11. Trial and judgment
12. Heavens and hells
13. Theory of transmigration
14. The deliverance and Mukti
15. The destination – Sach Khand
16. The route to Sach Khand through the inroads of dharam khand, gyan khand, saram khand and karam khand
17. The objectives of life

Musical Measures - Ragas, Raginis and Raga-sons

The basic theory of music classifies Music Measures into Ragas, Raginis (Raga-wives) and Raga-sons. Guru Granth Sahib has made no such distinction in listing ragas. It has used word Raga for all of them.

A Raga is a particular set of seven svars, or a selection of them, in their natural, sharp and soft forms, whose inter-relationship and sequence are governed by strict rules. Each raga has its own emotional character, and is associated with a particular time of the day and a particular period of a season.

The ragas facilitate 'Mood' variation through the seasons and the time of the day.

All compositions of Guru Granth Sahib are classified into different ragas except Japji in the beginning and Sloaks and Swayas at the end.

The ragas used in Guru Granth Sahib, their time and season of singing, status in the Ragamala and page numbers are as follows:

The name of the raga	Timing-pehr	Timing a.m./p.m.	Season-name	Season-months	Pages in Guru Granth Sahib	Status of raga as in raga-mala
1. Sri	Third pehr of the day	12-3 p.m.	Winter (hement)	Nov-Dec	14-93 (80)	Raga
2. Maj	Third pehr of the day	12-3 p.m.	Rainy (varsha)	July-Aug	94-151 (58)	Not mentioned
3. Gauri	Third pehr of the day	12-3 p.m.	Winter (shisher)	Dec-Jan	152-347 (196)	Ragini
4. Asa	Fourth pehr of the night	3 -6 a.m.	Winter (hement)	Nov-Dec	348-488 (141)	Ragini
5. Gujri	Fourth pehr of the day	3-6 p.m.	Rainy (varsha)	July-Aug	489-526 (38)	Ragini
6. Devgandhari	First pehr of the day	6-9 a.m.	Winter (shisher)	Dec-Jan	527-536 (10)	Ragini

7.	Bihagra	Second pehr of the night	9-12 p.m.	Winter (hement)	Nov-Dec	537-556 (20)	Not mentioned
8.	Wadhans	Fourth pehr of the day	3 -6 p.m.	Winter (shisher)	Dec-Jan	557-594 (38)	Not mentioned
9.	Sorath	Third pehr of the night	12-3 a.m.	Winter (sharad)	Oct-Nov	595-659 (65)	Ragini
10.	Dhanasri	Third pehr of the day	12-3 p.m.	Winter (shisher)	Dec-Jan	660-695 (36)	Ragini
11.	Jaitsiri	Third pehr of the day	12-3 p.m.	Winter (shisher)	Dec-Jan	696-710 (15)	Not mentioned
12.	Todi	First pehr of the day	6-9 a.m.	Winter (shisher)	Dec-Jan	711-718 (8)	Ragini
13.	Berari	Third pehr of the day	12-3 p.m.	Winter (sharad)	Oct-Nov	719-720 (2)	Ragini
14.	Tilang	Third pehr of the day	12-3 p.m.	Rainy (varsha)	July-Aug	721-727 (7)	Ragini
15.	Suhi	First pehr of the day	6-9 a.m.	Spring (basant)	Feb-Mar	728-794 (67)	Not mentioned
16.	Bilawal	First pehr of the day	6-9 a.m.	Spring (basant)	Feb-Mar	795-858 (64)	Raga-son
17.	Gaund	Third pehr of the day	12-3 p.m.	Winter (hement)	Nov-Dec	859-875 (17)	Raga-son
18.	Ramkali	First pehr of the day	6-9 a.m.	Spring (basant)	Feb-Mar	876-974 (99)	Not mentioned
19.	Nut Narain	Third pehr of the night	12-3 a.m.	Rainy (varsha)	July-Aug	975-983 (9)	Raga-son
20.	Mali Gaura	Third pehr of the day	12-3 p.m.	Winter (sharad)	Oct-Nov	984-988 (5)	Not mentioned
21.	Maru	Third pehr of the day	12-3 p.m.	Winter (shisher)	Dec-Jan	989-1106 (118)	Raga-son
22.	Tukhari	First pehr of the day	6-9 a.m.	Winter (sharad) (11)	Oct-Nov	1107-1117	Not mentioned
23.	Kedara	Fourth pehr of the day	3-6 p.m.	Summer (grikham)	May-Jun	1118-1124 (7)	Raga-son
24.	Bhairav	Fourth pehr of the night	3-6 a.m.	Winter (sharad)	Oct-Nov	1125-1167 (43)	Raga

25.	Basant	All times		Spring (basant)	Feb-Mar	1168-1196 (29)	Raga-son
26.	Sarang	Second pehr of the day	9-12 a.m.	Rainy (varsha)	July-Aug	1197-1253 (57)	Raga-son
27.	Malhar	All times		Rainy (varsha)	July-Aug	1254-1293 (40)	Ragini
28.	Kanra	First pehr of the night	6-9 p.m.	Summer (grikham)	May-Jun	1294-1318 (25)	Raga-son
29.	Kalyan	Fourth pehr of the day	3-6 p.m	Rainy (varsha)	July-Aug	1319-1326 (8)	Raga-son
30.	Parbhati	First pehr of the day	6-9 a.m.	Spring (basant)	Feb-Mar	1327-1351 (15)	Not mentioned
31.	Jaijaiwant	First pehr of the night	6-9 p.m.	Summer (grikham)	May-Jun	1352-1353 (2)	Not mentioned

At the end of Guru Granth Sahib, there is given a list of popular Indian ragas titled 'Ragamala'. Its author is not known. It has names of 6 ragas, 30 raginis and 48 raga-sons. Some of these ragas/raginis/raga-sons are used in Guru Granth Sahib as ragas. There are also ten ragas used in Guru Granth Sahib which are not mentioned in the ragamala. In this context ragamala should be called a list of ragas and not an index of ragas used in Guru Granth Sahib. The Indian music books have mentioned 10 different type of ragamala. The ragamala listed in Guru Granth Sahib is one of them.

Reference of additional ragas, mixed with 31 ragas, used in Guru Granth Sahib

Table
Six additional ragas

Name of raga	General Status	Names of the raga mixed with	Status as mentioned in the ragamala	One example, page number/s
Kaafi*	Ragini	Asa, Tilang, Suhi, Maru	Not mentioned	Page 369
Asawari	Ragini	Raga Asa	Ragini	Page 369
Lalit	Ragini	Raga Suhi	Raga-son	Page 793
Hindol	Raga	Raga Basant	Raga	Page 1171
Bhopali	Ragini	Raga Kalyan	Not mentioned	Page 1321
Vibhas	Ragini	Raga Parbhati	Not mentioned	Page 1327

*The word Kaafi also refers to the structure of a composition rather than a raga. In the early Punjabi literature, there are a number of Kaafis composed by Muslim writers viz., Shah Hussain and Bulle Shah. At sacred tombs Muslim singers, normally, recite Kaafis and Qwalis.

Rhythm - Ghars (Tal)

In music, harmonium (Piano) is normally accompanied with tabla (drums). The word *Tal* refers to the play of tabla (drums). It means rhythm, it also denotes the pitch of notes. It is a rhythmic cycle, comprising of a fixed number of time units (matras) of equal value.

In Guru Granth Sahib, Guru Arjan has used 17 different *Tals* which he calls *Ghars*.

The counting of 17 *ghars* (tal) in relation to basic music svars is done in the following way:

a. The basic svars in the Indian music are seven
    Sa Re Ga Ma Pa Dha Ni Sa

b. Two svars out of above seven are fixed viz., Sa and Pa

c. The remaining five svars are changing svars and can be played as follows:

Svar	1	2	3
Re	lower flat	flat	natural = 3
Ga	lower flat	flat	natural = 3
Da	lower flat	flat	natural = 3
Ni	lower flat	flat	natural = 3
Ma	sharp	very sharp	natural = 3

Total = 15
Fixed svars = 2
Grand total = 17

The Invocation - Mangal

Mangal is a Sanskrit word and it means a short prayer. It is recited/said before the start of any work. In Guru Granth Sahib five different types of mangals have been used, Their classification and location is as follows:

ੴ — Used only once at page 1353, before the start of second Sahaskriti sloak of Guru Nanak. New editions of Guru Granth Sahib do not record this.

ੴ ਸਤਿ ਗੁਰ ਪ੍ਰਸਾਦਿ ॥ Used 519 times: 5 chapter headings (Ragas: Sri, Jaitsiri, Berari, Tukhari and Kedara) and 514 various sub-headings

ੴ ਸਤਿ ਨਾਮੁ ਗੁਰ ਪ੍ਰਸਾਦਿ ॥ Used only 2 times as follows:
Raga Sri, page 81, Shabad Wanjara
Raga Bihagra, page 544
Chhant of Guru Arjan 4/1/4

ੴ ਸਤਿ ਨਾਮੁ ਕਰਤਾ ਪੁਰਖੁ ਗੁਰ ਪ੍ਰਸਾਦਿ ॥ Used 9 times as follows:
Maj di Var, page 137
Gauri Ashtpadi, page 220
Gauri Gurareri Ashtpadi, page 235
Gauri Purbi Chhant, pages 242, 243
Gauri Bhagta di bani, pages 323,345
Gauri Purbi Bawan akhri, page 340
Bilawal Bhagat di bani, page 855

ੴ ਸਤਿ ਨਾਮੁ ਕਰਤਾ ਪੁਰਖੁ ਨਿਰਭਉ ਨਿਰਵੈਰੁ ਅਕਾਲ ਮੂਰਤਿ ਅਜੂਨੀ ਸੈਭੰ ਗੁਰ ਪ੍ਰਸਾਦਿ ॥
Used 33 times as follows:
26 = at the start of raga chapters.
 1 = Start of Guru Granth Sahib.
 2 = additional in raga Asa,
Start of Asa di var, page 462
Start of Bhagat Bani, page 475
 1 = Sloak Sahakriti M: 1, page 1354
 1 = Sloak Sahaskriti M:5, page 1354
 1 = Sloak Varan tae vadeek, page 1410
 1 = Swayas Mehla 5, page 1385

*Please note that all Mangals, except the first one, have three words in common i.e., ੴ, ਸਤਿ and ਗੁਰ ਪ੍ਰਸਾਦਿ ॥ Hindu and Muslim scriptures have also used mangals to start a chapter/para.

The Theme and *Sthai* Verse of a composition – the Rahau verse/s

Meaning:

The title rahau refers to that verse, which contains the theme of the composition. It also refers to the verse which the ragis (singers of Gurbani) are supposed to repeat after every 'antra' of the composition.

Rahau is not a punctuation symbol as is understood by a number of scholars. It is the title of the core verse/s in a composition.

Most of the compositions in the 'Raga section' (pages 14 – 1353) of Guru Granth Sahib have a rahau verse in them, and there are example of compositions with one, two, three, four and six rahau verses.

If a composition has two rahaus, then the first rahau verse poses a thematic question and the second verse contains the answer to the question posed.

If a composition has three rahaus, then the first rahau would contain a thematic advice, the second rahau would state the limitations or difficulties to be encountered by the devotees and the last rahau would suggest the way to realise the goal based on the theme of the composition.

Where there are more than three rahaus, there each rahau verse would describe the theme of the preceding pada (stanza).

It is important to know the placing and numbering of rahau verses to understand their significance in a composition. For practical explanation the following text and examples of hymns from Guru Granth Sahib are produced.

Placement of rahau verse/s in a composition:

The single rahau verse has either been placed in the beginning of a composition or after the end of the first pada of the composition.

Where there are two rahaus the second rahau is placed at the end of the shabad and it ends with the text number 'Rahau dooja'.

Where there are three or more rahau verses in a composition, they have been spread throughout the composition.

Numerical reference of rahau/s in a composition:

At many places number [1] is used before the rahau title, and at other places such a number has not been used.

Whether a composition has one or more than one rahau verse, the number with each rahau verse is always [1], except where there are two rahaus, in such a case, as referred above, the second rahau has a text title which reads 'rahau dooja'.

It must be noted that the rahau verse/s is/are not counted in the total count of verses in a composition.

The number of rahau/s verses in a composition:

As stated above there are examples of one, two, three, four, and six rahaus in Guru Granth Sahib. While there is only one shabad with six rahaus (Wanjara in raga Sri, page 81-82), probably one shabad with three rahau verses (page 154/155 (13)), four shabads with four rahau verses [pages 16 – 17 (7), 96 –97 (8), 356 (26) 660 (1)] and probably 19 shabads with two rahau verses, pages: 176 (**), 179 (81), 182 (89) , 204/205 (122), 371 (4), 374 (12), 384 (52), 385 (58), 403 (126), 624 (61), 642 (3), 687 (3) 738 (5) (7) (two shabads), 877 (3), 886 (12), 1002 (11), 1003 (15), and 1348 (second ashtpadi) the remaining shabads, where relevant, have only one rahau verse in them.

** This is the first shabad which ends on page 176, but its number is not given in Guru Granth Sahib. Where the shabad preceding this shabad is given cumulative number 70, the shabad which follows it is given the number 71.

The only shabad with three rahaus is found on page 155 (shabad 13).

The only shabad with six rahau verses is on pages 81-82.

The location of rahau verses in the three sections of Guru Granth Sahib

Rahau verses have been used only in those compositions which have been assembled under raga titles i.e., section II (pages 14 – 1353), and all those nitnem-section shabads, section I, which have been selected from the raga section. There are no rahau verses in the concluding section i.e., section III.

Compositions which are in raga chapters, section II, but which do not have rahau verses in them, are:

1. Vars (Except Var Ramkali page 947 pauri 1 which has a rahau verse)

2. Chhants (except one Chhant page 1122 which has a rahau verse in it)

3. In raga Maj none of the shabads (chaupadas) have rahau verses in them, except one shabad which has four rahau verses. All ashtpadis (except two ashtpadis of Guru Arjan Dev), however, have rahau verses in them.

4. Sloaks which have been included:
    i.   In the 'Nitnem section' in Japji
    ii.   In the 'Raga section' in twenty Vars, in Chhants of Guru Arjan and in a few specialist compositions, and
    iii. In the concluding section

    have no rahau verse in them except one Sloak of Guru Nanak, page 469, which is included in Asa di var, preceding pauri 12.

The Three sections of Guru Granth Sahib and the rahau verses:

Section 1

Nitnem Section: (pages 1-13)

Japji has no rahau verse in it.

All other shabads: Sodar (5 shabads), Sopurkh (4 shabads) and Sohila (5 shabads) are taken from the raga section of Guru Granth Sahib and have rahau verses in them.

Section 2

Raga Section (pages 14 – 1353)

Most of the compositions of 31 raga chapters have rahau verses in them except chaupada

28

compositions in raga Majh which have no rahau verses in them (save one shabad of Guru Arjan Dev, 'mera man lochae Gur darshan taene….') and a few other exceptions mentioned above and hereunder.

Section 3

Concluding Section: (pages 1354 – 1430)

None of the compositions in this section have rahau verses in them.

Specialist Banis in Guru Granth Sahib and the inclusion of rahau verses in them:

1. Jap ji (pages 1 –8) has no rahau verse.
2. Sodar shabad[1] (pages 6, 8, 347-348) has no rahau verse.
3. Sopurkh shabad (pages 10 – 11, 348) has no rahau verse.
4. Baramah (pages 133 - 136, 1107) has no rahau verse.
5. Din rein (pages 136 – 137) has no rahau verse.
6. Bawan Akhri (250 – 262) has one rahau verse at the end of the first pauri.
7. Sukhmani (pages 262 – 296) has 24 Ashtpadis but has only one rahau verse in the first ashtpadi placed at the end of first pada.
8. Thithe (pages 296 – 300) has one rahau verse at the end of the first pauri.
9. Patti (pages 432 – 434) has one rahau verse at the end of the first pada.
10. Anand (pages 917 – 922) has no rahau verse.
11. Ruti (pages 927 – 929) has no rahau verse.
12. Dakhni Onkar (pages 929 – 938) has one rahau verse at the end of the first pada.
13. Sidh Ghost (pages 938 – 946) has one rahau verse at the end of the first pada.

---

[1]   In the 'nitnem section' titles ' Sodar' and 'Sopurkh' are used for both a cluster of shabads and solo shabads of the similar names. The solo shabads Sodar and Sopurkh have no rahau verses in them, whereas other shabads under those group titles do have rahau verses in them.

Counting of Hymns – the Numerical System

In Guru Granth Sahib, there is a very sophisticated system of counting hymns. To understand the system the following two points are to be noted:

1. The first number always signifies padas (stanzas) in the last shabad, and

2. the last number always signifies the cumulative total of all shabads under that heading. (these two rules are fixed, whereas other rules change frequently)

    For example if a Shabad has a number 4/5 then it means:
    4 = four padas in the last Shabad
    5 = total shabads so far.

3. When a heading or subheading changes, the numerical system start afresh.

4. In raga Sri (the first raga), when Guru Nanak's shabads end the number is 4/33, which
    means: 4 = number of padas in the last Shabad,
                   33 = total shabads of Guru Nanak

5. In the same raga when Guru Amardas's Shabad ends, the number is 4/31/64 which means:
                    4 = number of padas in the last Shabad
                   31 = number of shabads of Guru Amardas
                   64 = cumulative total of shabads of both Gurus

6. When Guru Ramdas's shabads end, the number is 4/33/31/6/70
    which means: 4 = number of padas in the last Shabad
                   33 = number of Guru Nanak's shabads
                   31 = number of Guru Amardas's shabads
                    6 = number of Guru Ramdas's shabads
                   70 = cumulative total of all shabads

    Please note the difference in numbering after Guru Amardas's shabads and Guru Ramdas's shabads. The fixed rules do not change, where the other rule has changed.

7. When Guru Arjan's shabads end the number is 4/30/100,
    which means: 4 = number of padas in the last Shabad

30 = number of Guru Arjan's shabads
100 = cumulative total of all shabads of all Gurus.

Please note the difference in numbering after Guru Amardas's, Guru Ramdas's and Guru Arjan's shabads. The fixed rules do not change, where the other rule has changed.

8. The above rules of counting apply throughout Guru Granth Sahib, but there are a number of exceptions to the rule which can be learnt by going through each chapter.

9. A new Numbering system start when chapter or para changes.

Arrangement of Hymns –
Horizontal and Vertical sequences

For study purposes, the text of Guru Granth Sahib can be divided into three sections, which are as follows:

1. First section, pages 1-13, the Nitnem Section.
2. Second section, pages 14-1353, the Raga Section, and
3. Third section, pages 1354 – 1430, the Concluding Section.

The arrangement of Bani in the three sections is as follows:

First Section:

The sequence is as follows:

a. Full Mool Mantra
b. Japji (Two sloaks and 38 stanzas called pauris)
c. Sodar (a collection of five shabads: 3 shabads of Guru Nanak, 1 shabad of Guru Ramdas and 1 shabad of Guru Arjan).
d. Sopurkh (a collection of four shabads: 1 shabad of Guru Nanak, 2 shabads of Guru Ramdas and 1 shabad of Guru Arjan). *This collection is not in the Kartarpuri Bir.*
e. Sohila (a collection of five shabads: 3 shabads of Guru Nanak, 1 shabad of Guru Ramdas and 1 shabad of Guru Arjan.

Second Section:

There are 31 Chapters each headed by a Raga. In each chapter the sequence of compositions is as follows:

Horizontal Sequence

1	2	3	4	5	6	7
Shabads 1-6 padas	Shabads 8 padas called **Ashtpadi**	Specialist Banis Titled/ untitled	Shabad Titled **Chhants**	Specialist BanisTitled/ untitled	Long Banis Titled **Vars**	Bhagat Bani

Guru Nanak
Guru Amardas
Guru Ramdas
Guru Arjan
Guru Tegh Bahadur

Vertical Sequence

Notes on the above sequences:

1. Guru Angad (Mehla 2) has not composed any shabads, Ahstpadis, Specialist compositions or Vars. He has composed only Sloaks which have been included in Vars. This is the reason that his name (Mehla 2) is not included in the vertical sequence of Guru composers.
2. In Bhagat bani wherever Farid's compositions have come in a raga, they have been included at the end of the Bhagat Bani. (see raga Asa page 488, raga Suhi page 794)
3. In Srirag compositions of Bhagats Trilochan and Beni have appeared before Ravidas, where Beni is recorded after Ravidas in raga Ramkali.
4. In raga Gujri compositions of Bhagats Trilochan and Jaidev are recorded after Ravidas
5. In raga Dhanasri again Bhagat Trilochan's compositions have come after Ravidas followed by Sain, Pipa and Dhanna.
6. In raga Maru composition of Jaidev is recorded before Ravidas (page 1106) whereas in raga Gujri it was recorded after Ravidas (page 526)
7. In raga Basant Bhagat Ramanand's composition has appeared before Namdev and Ravidas (page 1195)
8. The sequence of Gurus is the same under each block i.e., 1-6

33

9. Though the title Ashtpadi means a composition of 8 padas, but there are compositions of less and more than 8 padas and still titled as Ashtpadis.
10. Lines in a pada are called 'Tukas'. Padas in the Chhants have more tukas than compositions in block 1 & 2.
11. The title 'Shabad' for block 1 compositions is used in raga Maru.
12. The above sequences have three exceptions: pages 347/348, 724-726, 1169 where there is change in the sequence in the Gurbani.

Third Section:
In the concluding section the sequence of compositions is as follows:

Composition	Composer	Page number
Sloak Sahaskriti	Guru Nanak	1353
Sloak Sahaskriti	Guru Arjan	1353 - 1360
Sloak - Gatha	Guru Arjan	1360 - 1361
Sloak - Phuney	Guru Arjan	1361-1363
Sloak - Chaubole	Guru Arjan	1363 - 1364
Sloak – Kabir	Kabir	1364 - 1377
Sloak – Farid	Farid	1377 - 1384
Swayas – Mukhvak Mehla 5	Guru Arjan	1384 - 1389
Swayas for Mehla 1	Bhatt Kal	1389 - 1390
Swayas for Mehla 2	Bhatt Kalshar	1391 - 1392
Swayas for Mehla 3	Bhatts: Kalshar, Jalap, Kirat, Bhikhey, Sal, Bhal	1392 - 1396
Swayas for Mehla 4	Bhatts: Kal, Kalshar, Kirat, Sal, Gayandh, Mathura, Bal	1396 - 1406
Swayas for Mehla 5	Bhatts: Kalshar, Mathura, Harbans	1406 - 1409
Sloak Varan te vadeek Mehlas 1,2,4,5,9	Guru Nanak, Guru Amardas Guru Ramdas Guru Arjan Guru Tegh Bahadur	1410 - 1412 1413 - 1421 1421 - 1424 1424 - 1426 1426 - 1429
Mundavni Sloak	Guru Arjan Guru Arjan	1429 1429
Ragamala	Not known	1429-1430

Segment 13

A Few points of Sikh Philosophy and Sikh Values

1. There is one God of the whole universe.
2. He controls the functioning of the universe from His palatial dwelling situated in the world unknown.
3. He is both *Nirgun* (He cannot be seen with human eyes) and *Sargun* (He can be seen with special powers given by His own Grace).
4. God is both accessible and approachable.
5. He lives in His own palace and can come to stay with His devotees as and when He wishes.
6. A specific relationship must be developed with Him to realise Him, and be with Him.
7. The realisation of God, and His visit in our lives destroy all grief and pain and brings in all sorts of happiness, comforts and satisfaction.
8. In order to talk to God, to make Him stay with us and have His blessings one must keep regular communication with Him (Nitnem, meditation, worship, prayers) and must live a truthful life (a life of honesty, compassion, humility, loyalty and devotion).
9. God has created this world of ours at His will. The exact date of its creation is not known. He has created countless other worlds as well.
10. The creation process, of the world, has been designed by God Himself and He may change it at His will.
11. Since the beginning of time, the world has been created and destroyed many a times.
12. Sikhs must perform their daily prayers with intensity, regularity, commitment and non-faltering belief in God.
13. Sikhs must live a pure, transparent, holy, honest and truthful life.
14. Sikhs must visit Gurdwara and join the sadh sangat for their prayers.
15. The company of Sadh sangat is of paramount importance for a Sikh.
16. The Gurdwara service includes, listening to kirtan/katha, joining in ardas, listening to hukamnama and partaking of langar.
17. Sikhs must believe that there is a life after death, the quality and format of which is determined and shaped according to karmas and meditation performed in this life. There is a repeated mention of 8.4 million lives.
18. Sikhs must believe that there are numerous heavens and hells in the world hereafter, where the soul goes according to the judgment pronounced in the Divine court. There is a repeated mention of 'Dharmraj' the agent who pronounces final judgement, and 'Chitar and Gupt' who record the karmas.
19. Sikhs must not believe in caste system and must not discriminate people on the basis of their colour, religion and nationality.

20. Sikhs should not believe in renunciation and celibacy. They believe in a householder's life. It is a happy home where God dwells.
21. The word Satguru refers to Waheguru.
22. The word Guru refers to Waheguru, the Sikh Gurus and a teacher-Guru, depending on the text of the Shabad.
23. For a Sikh the real 'Jog' is a householder's life.
24. A Sikh is not to undergo any body penances to realise God, meditation and good deeds are the only requirements to realise God.
25. There are no restrictions on partaking any food, except that a Sikh must not eat '*Kutha*' (Halal, Kosher) meat (refer to Sikh rehat Maryada), and the food which inflames one's passions (refer to Guru Nanak in raga Sri).
26. A Sikh may live a luxurious life, provided he/she does not forget God and His commandments as recorded in Guru Granth Sahib.
27. A Sikh must believe in the unity of God, the teachings of the Sikh Gurus, the sovereignty of Guru Granth Sahib and the necessity of *'Khande di pahul'* (the Sikh baptism ceremony)
28. A Sikh must believe and accept in the 'Hukam' and live within its orbit.

Segment 14

An Analysis of specialist compositions

WHICH HAVE A TITLE

No.	Page No.	Name of Bani	Composer	STRUCTURE				
				Shabads	Ashtpadis	Padas	Pauris	Sloaks
1.	1-8	Jap	Guru Nanak				38	2
2.	8-10	Sodar	Guru Nanak	3				
			Guru Ramdas	1				
			Guru Arjan	1				
3.	10-11	Sopurakh	Guru Nanak	1				
			Guru Ramdas	2				
			Guru Arjan	1				
4.	11-12	Sohila	Guru Nanak	3				
			Guru Ramdas	1				
			Guru Arjan	1				
5.	74-78	Pehre	Guru Nanak	5		4/5/4/5 = 18		
6.	81	Wanjara	Guru Ramdas			6		
7.	133	Baramah	Guru Arjan	14				
8.	136	Din Rein	Guru Arjan			4		
9.	234	Karhale	Guru Ramdas	2		10/10 = 20		
10.	250	Bawan Akhri	Guru Arjan				55	57
11.	262	Sukhmani	Guru Arjan		24			24
12.	296	Thithe	Guru Arjan				17	17
13.	340	Bawan Akhri	Kabir			45		
14.	432	Patti Likhi	Guru Nanak			38		

15.	434	Patti	Guru Amardas			18		
16.	575	Ghoreaan	Guru Ramdas			4		
17.	578	Allahian	Guru Nanak	5		4/4/4/4 4 = 20		
18.	762	Kuchaji	Guru Nanak			1		
19.	762	Suchaji	Guru Nanak			1		
20.	763	Gunwanti	Guru Nanak			· 1		
21.	838	Thithe	Guru Nanak			20		
22.	841	Var	Guru Amardas			10/10=20		
23.	917	Anand	Guru Amardas				40	
24.	923	Sud	Baba Sundar			6		
25.	927	Rutti	Guru Arjan			8/chhants		16
26.	929	Dakhni Onkar	Guru Nanak			54		
27.	938	Sidh Gosht	Guru Nanak			73		
28.	1107	Baramah	Guru Nanak	17				
29.	1110	Pehre	Guru Nanak			5		
30.	1360	Gatha	Guru Arjan			24		
31.	1361	Phune	Guru Arjan			23		
32.	1363	Chaubole	Guru Arjan			11		

An Analysis of different types of Compositions

According to one count there are 5894 hymns in Guru Granth Sahib. The split of hymns in different categories of compositions is as follows:

The category	The count
One pada (stanza) compositions	5 (2 shabads and 3 titled compositions)
Two pada compositions	608
Three pada compositions	73
Four pada compositions	1255
Five pada compositions	80
Six pada compositions	11
Eight pada compositions (called Ashtpadis)	311
Sixteen pada compositions	62
Specialist compositions	130, of which 32 are titled compositions
Chhants (Compositions of special praises)	144
Vars (ballads)	22
Swayas (compositions of undefined length)	143 (of which 20 are composed by Guru Arjan and 123 by Bhhats)
Sloaks (couplets)	1659

The count of compositions as per different composers is as follows:

The Composer/revelation recipient	The count
Guru Nanak	974
Guru Angad	63
Guru Amardas	907
Guru Ramdas	679
Guru Arjan	2218
Guru Tegh Bahadur	115

15 Bhagats	937
11 Bhhats	123
4 Other devotees	One var (Satta & Balwand), 3 sloaks (Bhai Mardana), one specialist (Baba Sundar)

An Analysis of Nitnem Banis
(Compositions which are recited by all practising Sikhs)

The analysis of the Nitnem Bani as recommended in the Sikh Rehat Marayad (The Book of Code of Conduct) is as follows:

The Composition	Composer	Page/s in the Scriptures	Time of recitation
Jap Ji (2 sloaks and 38 pauris)	Handed personally by God to Guru Nanak	1-8 Guru Granth Sahib (GGS)	Morning
Jap Sahib (199 hymns_	Guru Gobind Singh	First chapter in Dasam Granth	Morning
Sudha Swayas (10 hymns)	Guru Granth Sahib Akal Ustat, Second chapter of Dasam Granth	Hymns 21-30 of	Morning
Sodar (Five Shabads)	Guru Nanak = 3 shabsdx Guru Ramdas = 1 shabad Guru Arjan = 1 shabad	8-10 Guru Granth Sahib	Evening
Sopurkh (Four shabads)	Guru Nanak =1 shabad Guru Ramdas = 2 shabad Guru Arjan = 1 shabad	10-12 Guru Granth Sahib	Evening
Benti Chaupai (25 verses)	Guru Gobind Singh	Verses 377-401 0f Chittaropakhayan, chapter 13 of Dasam Granth	Evening
One Swaya	Guru Gobind Singh	Verse 863 of Ram Avtar, chapter 8 of Dasam Granth	Evening

One Doha	Guru Gobind Singh	Verse 864 of Ram Avtar, chapter 8 of Dasam Granth	Evening
Six pauris of Anand Sahib	Guru Amardas		Evening
Mundavni Sloak Pauri Sloak Sloak	Guru Arjan Guru Arjan Guru Arjan Guru Arjan Guru Arjan	page 1429 (GGS) page 1429 page 961-962 517 517	Evening Evening
Sohila (5 shabads)	Guru Nanak = 3 Guru Ramdas = 1 Guru Arjan = 1	Pages 12-13	Bed time

42

Guru Granth Sahib in the eyes of non-Sikh Writers

Dr. Arnold J. Toynbee – a British historian[2]

"Mankind's religious future may be obscure; yet, one thing can be forseen: the living higher religions are going to influence each other more than ever before, in these days of increasing communication between all parts of the world and all branches of the human race. In this religious debate, the Sikh religion, and its scripture the Adi Granth, will have something of special value to say the rest."

Pearl S. Buck – an American Noble Prize laureate[3]

"I have studied the scriptures of other great religions, but I do not find elsewhere the same power of appeal to the heart and mind as I feel here, in the words of Guru Granth Sahib".

J.C. Archer – a prominent British writer[4]

"The religion of Guru Granth Sahib, is a universal and practical religion. The world needs today its message of peace and love."

Dr. Duncam Greenlees – an eminent British scholar[5]

"Guru Granth Sahib is Guru's (God's) own book through which he has been talking to his devotees for ages."

Rabindra Nath Tagore – a Noble Prize laureate[6]

"What makes the songs of Guru Granth Sahib a great poetry, is the whole radiance and purity of their emotion, absolutely untrammeled by the pettifogging dogmas of concentional theology."

Dr. S Radhakrishanan – an eminent philosopher and President of India[7]

"The word of the guru is the music which the seers hear in their moments of ecstasy: the word of the guru is the highest scripture. By communion with the word we attain the vision unattainble. ……we find in the Adi Granth a wide range of mystical emotion, infinite expressions of the personal realization of God and rapturous hymns of divine love…"

Swami Ram Tirath – an eminent saint[8]

"…Nowhere, in the other scriptures, I have come across the hymns of the quality matching the hymns of Guru Granth Sahib…"

---

2 Selection from the Sacred Writings of the Sikhs, page 9
3 Introduction - Translation of Guru Granth Sahib by Dr. Gopal Singh, page XIX
4 A study in comparative religion.
5 Abstracts of Sikh Studies Volume V, Issue I, page 86
6 Autobiography.
7 Indian Philosophy
8 The supreme Scripture Adi Sri Guru Granth Sahib

Professor T Krishna Nathan – Professsor at Madurai Kamaraj University Madurai[9]

"Guru Granth Sahib, the religious scripture of the Sikhs is the ocean of spiritual and human values entrusted to the Sikhs to celebrate and cherish to learn and follow, to spread and educate the humanity. It glorifies God and the world, makes people aware of the socio-cultural situations into which the people are thrown. Guru Granth Sahib renders valuable guidelines to live and better the world..........It contains a unique philosophy of post medieval period that had withstood the challenges of even the modern period."

Professor Abdul Majid Khan[10] - Vice Chancellor Aligarh Muslim University.

"Baba Nanak was a prophet of universal love, a light-house for the whole humanity, a redeemer of all mankind.......The message in Guru Granth Sahib deals with the task of emancipating human beings from the yoke of oppression, injustice, superstition and falsehood...and Guru Nanak, the Divine Master, was revealed this word..."

Dr. Mohammed Iqbal – A great Poet and Philosopher[11]

"Call for uncompromising monotheistic renaissance has again risen from Punjab. A supreme being (Guru Nanak) has awakened India from slumber."

ਫਿਰ ਉਠੀ ਆਖਰ ਸਦਾ ਤੌਹੀਦ ਕੀ ਪੰਜਾਬ ਸੇ
ਹਿੰਦ ਕੋ ਇੱਕ ਮਰਦਿ-ਕਾਮਲ ਨੇ ਜਗਾਇਆ ਖਾਬ ਸੇ ॥

"Sikhism, in fact, is higher Islam for it endlessly glorifies the Merciful aspect of God...."

Professor Dr. Klaus Bruhn, Indologist, Free University of Berlin, Germany

Guru Nanak – Lightstripes

Guru Nanak's annunciation is an unending talk with God. This God is not a nameless God of mysticism in which the believer countersinks to be one with Him. God stands in front of the men, who put questions to Him and also ask themselves whether they live according to His will.

Professor Dr. Hans Braeker, Indologist, University of Trier, Germany

The "God teacher" Nanak, a spiritual Revolutionary in India

God revealed to Guru Nanak that religions do not make a difference between human beings, they are all equal irrespective of their religious belief and caste. He introduced the custom of Community Kitchen. Sikhs sat together with their Teacher Nanak at the same level. This act was an unbelievable deed because it meant a direct breach of the Caste System Commandments.

Professor Dr. Jaroslav Poncar, Publicist, University of Koeln, Germany

My meetings with the "Lions" from Punjab

On the Baisakhi day in 1699 the caste system was abolished for the Sikhs. Since then all male members of Sikh religion are called *Singh – the Lion* and all female members are called *Kaur – Princess*. This day is celebrated every year as the Name Day of all *Singhs* and *Kaurs*.

---

9   Importance of the teachings of Sri Guru Granth Sahib in Present Era

10   The Punjab of Guru Nanak

11   Modern Review, Calcutta